PRAISE FOR

Opening Thoughts on Everyday Living
Digging Deeper, Looking Farther

"When you discover that a friend who works for justice and peace is also a contemplative writer it is a wonderful surprise! Don Welch has spent a career teaching and advocating. Now he is publishing his first book of reflections and poetry. This book is beautiful and it calls us all to stop and see that where we are is in a holy moment. Don is a gift. And Don's writing is a gift. Give yourself a gift and take the time to read it!"

— THE REV. BECCA STEVENS, FOUNDER OF MAGDALENE AND
THISTLE FARMS

"With *Opening Thoughts on Everyday Living,* Don Welch demonstrates what an underappreciated, meditative act it is to direct our attention to our words, and what they might mean, and what they point to. Maybe in your reading you'll experience a slowing of your breath, like I did, as Don's marvelous "Opening Thoughts" lead you into a place of thoughtful kindness. And maybe, like me, you'll find yourself moved to take a walk afterwards and noticing that your attention is heightened, your mind more playful. Attention is a magical thing, and I guess that makes Don Welch a magician for directing ours to such wondrous spaces of the heart."

— DAVID HUTCHENS, AUTHOR OF *CIRCLE OF THE NINE MUSES:*
A STORYTELLING FIELD GUIDE FOR INNOVATORS AND MEANING
MAKERS

"I love this book. Like the "Opening Thoughts" it includes, it defies easy description. It is a wise, whimsical, poignant, and profound collection of anecdotes, observations, musings, meditations, poems, stories, and songs. It captures much about one man's inner life, and in so doing, it provides universal insights. Slow down and enjoy."

— CHRIS GUTHRIE, DEAN, VANDERBILT UNIVERSITY LAW SCHOOL

"In *Opening Thoughts on Everyday Living*, Don Welch offers consistently wise, clear views on everyday living. This book offers a clarion call for those of us who want to see, listen, and *be* in a world that's often begging for and competing for our attention. Dwell in Welch's awareness for a little while; I promise you won't be sorry!"
— BONNIE SMITH WHITEHOUSE, DIRECTOR OF HONORS AND PROFESSOR OF ENGLISH, BELMONT UNIVERSITY, AUTHOR OF *AFOOT AND LIGHT HEARTED*

"In *Opening Thoughts on Everyday Living*, Don Welch turns those fast food sound bites so beloved in the South inside out and upside down. In the process, this kind and thoughtful gentleman serves them back to us as a five-star meal that reminds us just how nourishing "small talk" can be when we mean what we say and say what we mean."
— HAL CATO, CEO OF THISTLE FARMS AND FOUNDER OF HANDS ON NASHVILLE

"I've known Don Welch for almost 50 years and have read much of what he's published, but this book surprised me. He is widely known for his insights, analytical skills, and clear writing, and here he also demonstrates an uncanny ability to step back, discern the niceties and oddities in our everyday worlds, and open up new ways of perceiving them. As he invites us to linger over them with him, he makes the process rewarding with his playful use of words and his poetic expressions. This book deserves to be read slowly and thoughtfully — again and again."
— DOUGLAS A. KNIGHT, DRUCILLA MOORE BUFFINGTON PROFESSOR OF HEBREW BIBLE EMERITUS AND PROFESSOR OF JEWISH STUDIES, VANDERBILT UNIVERSITY

"Don Welch shares his personal thoughts and struggles using humor, poetry, imagery, metaphors and more. In doing so useful suggestions emerge as guiding points for one's life journey and he offers much that touches one's spirit and mind."
— REV. DR. ROBERTO GÓMEZ

Opening Thoughts on Everyday Living

Digging Deeper, Looking Farther

Don Welch

ISBN: 978-1-953865-36-6 (Paperback)
ISBN: 978-1-953865-37-3 (eBook)
Library of Congress Control Number: 2021912745

Books Fluent
3014 Dauphine Street
New Orleans, LA
70117

To my

wild and wonderful

family

Contents

INTRODUCTION 7

HEARD 11

SEEN 49

THOUGHT 89

SUNG 127

POSTSCRIPT 141

Introduction

We live in a sound bite world. All too often, our public conversation is reduced to sound bites, which are really no conversation at all. They are regularly used as weapons in culture wars or to boost ratings. Sound bites are a particularly prominent example of the shortcuts, available to all of us, that provide us with a way to avoid hard thinking. They are simple, easy to remember, and are never the whole story.

Increasingly, our public discourse consists of throwing slogans and epithets back and forth. The image that comes to mind is two children in a playground argument, shouting at each other: "Is not!" and "Is too!" Sound bites and their kin are blurbs used for their attention-grabbing power, not for their informational value. They are superficial—hitting a quick lick and then moving on. They sometimes work because our societal attention span is short.

I provide an alternative in this book, in the form of what I'm calling Opening Thoughts. These pieces are designed to encourage a lingering with a subject—fostering a more substantive consideration of the issue at hand.

This book is an invitation to look below surfaces and beyond first appearances. As I was assembling my reflections that make up these Opening Thoughts (stories, essays, poems, songs, and other observations), I noticed a recurring feature. I realized that I had been attempting, in those writings, to expand my understanding of the world in which we live. Just as I had tried to provoke students to think during all of those years teaching in the classroom, in these writings I was provoking myself to think more. I was try-ing to dig more deeply into what I have heard, what I have seen, and what I have thought.

This book presents its invitation through example, not through directives about how you should proceed or what conclusions you should draw. You are just invited to look through these exhibits, which are by and large personal reflections, and see what thoughts open to you.

I have been told that it is good to read this book one or two pieces at a time. One reader suggested reading some of the pieces twice— once in the morning, and again that evening. This approach makes sense; after all, the intention here is to go deeper and look farther. That said, I also know some very thoughtful people who take long strides and cover distances swiftly. Whether you take it in bit by bit or all at once, may your pace lead you to a satisfying reading experience.

In a sound bite world, we are tempted to take shortcuts, to replace our own searching with pre-packaged answers and preferences. Examples include:

 —Everyone knows . . .

 —My teacher said . . .

 —I have always believed . . .

 —It's the way I was raised.

Let's not surrender our own judgement to parents or children, or teachers, preachers, bosses, talking heads, politicians, or AUTHORS.

You are invited to join me on this journey. *Opening Thoughts* might provide a starting place, but after that you are on your own. This can be a journey in which we declare ourselves to be open

to something like a pilgrimage—a pilgrimage on which we seek
to hear another lesson, to see another revelation, to understand
another point of view. Along the way, we might even sing a new
song.

Heard

Words matter.

I learned a lesson about words at an early age.

I was about eight years old when Uncle Bill asked me to be his baseball team's batboy. With great anticipation, I rode with him out to the Cascades ballfield. My dreams were shattered when I found out that batboys take care of the bats. They do not get to bat.

We need to pay attention to words. To listen carefully. To explore again and again what words can mean. To wander through what we hear.

And, to strive unceasingly to find the words that advance our quest to express our own thoughts and feelings and beliefs—all of which are beyond complete capture.

Taking Care

"Take care," I often say, when a friend and I go our separate ways. These parting words once seemed like little more than a shopworn cliché—until I spent some time reflecting on the meanings that these two words can bear.

Take Care.

The phrase can mean be careful, it's a dangerous world out there. It can be an admonition or a reminder that you should be alert, aware, and protect yourself. Pay attention and protect yourself from all sorts of injury or accident or illness that could do you harm.

In a similar vein, taking care can also counsel against doing harm to yourself. Avoid mistakes or poor judgments. Be careful not to be too rash; also, be careful not to be too timid or too fearful. Employ good judgment in your decisions and actions, so that you do not inflict injury upon yourself.

I confess that I have not always been a big fan of the recent "self-care" movement. My initial resistance was rooted in a concern that many folks were already too busy taking care of themselves, at the expense of (or at least with a lack of interest in) others who need care. However, over time I have come to a greater appreciation of the need for caring for oneself, especially when it increases one's capacity to take care of others. So yes, take care of yourself.

And also take care of others. The kinds of mistakes and poor judgments that can inflict harm upon yourself can also inflict harm upon others. So, avoid actions or words that do harm to others. From there, it is only a small step to a more positive word of counsel: taking care can also embrace taking care *to* others, as in delivering care to others. If we exhort friends to avoid harming others, would we not also wish for them to be alert to opportunities to do good for others? An exhortation to go forth and do good.

Here is one final pass at unpacking meanings for "Take Care" . . .

I have, seemingly by accident, developed a rather silly habit. This habit is often on display on an uneven or rocky hiking trail, but it can even show up on a level floor. A friend slips or stumbles, and I reflexively reach out and instinctively say "Careful!" Of course, the words and action are hardly helpful, which is why it is a silly gesture. She already knows to be careful, and the helping hand is rarely helpful because it is usually unneeded or extended too late . . . after the need has passed. Unhelpful. A silly reflex. Except as it takes on one additional form of Taking Care. My favorite form.

Take my care with you. When I say Take Care, increasingly I think of it as passing along my good wishes. In essence, know that I care for you. I am hoping for the best for you. I am invested in your well-being, and I care about how things go for you. I want you to be well and to do well.

So, y'all take care now, ya hear?

CHAINSAWS

Pushing a stroller full of granddaughter
A chainsaw roars to life, terminating her nap.
I was already irritated by those repeated roars
breaking our neighborhood's peace.
Too often another tree
had been declared to be disposable.

Another place, another time:
an army of chainsaws with their masters
poured into the tornado's wake.
They went to work on broken trees,
shattered trees, splintered trees,
trees on roofs, trees in roofs.
Residents' lives disrupted by those trees.

Chainsaws . . . just like people
You can judge the noise they make
By the purposes they serve.

Gay and I were married for 23 years; we raised four children and remain good friends. I recall the time when we knew we needed a bigger house. We received the news that we were going to be adding a third child to our family in about seven months. The news was delivered five months after we had brought home child number two. If you're trying to do the math in your head, yes, their birthdays ended up being less than a year apart. Did I mention that the "oldest" child would be three years old when her second sibling arrived?

Deciding that we needed more space was not a long, drawn-out process. Nothing drastic like moving, just enlarging the kitchen and adding a room to the back of the house. Along the way, my parents offered to lend us the money that would make it all possible. What a gift!

The completed addition gave us breathing space that enhanced the life of our family. After a while, we told my parents we were ready to begin repaying the loan. They turned us down. They told us to apply that first year's loan repayment to our family bills. We did, and when the next year rolled around, we again said we were ready to start the repayment process. Again, they turned us down.

My dad said that he had recently given some financial assistance to each of my brothers. He said that he and mom didn't need the repayment dollars yet. He was keeping track of the loans in a little black book, and when the time came that they did need us to repay that money, he would let us know. This gift was not given out of financial abundance. They lived for over fifty years in the modest house where they raised their children. Our most amazing family vacation, taken in my pre-teen years, was a train trip from South Texas to Seattle. Decades later, I learned that they financed that trip by taking out a loan on my dad's life insurance policy, a loan that was repaid over a twenty-year period. His money finally did run out; in his last months, my brothers and I helped with his bills.

Dad outlived Mom. So, when he died, we cleaned out the family home and sold the house. As we started that task, we kept an eye out for the little black book. As we went through each room, as we emptied the contents of each drawer and shelf and cabinet, the book was on our minds. Then, the moment arrived when we had handled every item in that house.

There was no black book. There never was a black book, and we think he never intended to start one.

Dad was not about justice; he was about grace. When it came to family, to his three sons (and sometimes other folks), he was not into careful calculations of what was deserved; he was into giving. The fact that there was no black book was a huge gift. For decades, little black books have been known as places to record exploits and conquests. He transformed that image into a means of grace that wiped our slates clean. Once we realized there was no black book, we went about our business—sorting through the last photographs and arranging the yard sale for the items that were left behind.

It was only much later that I reflected on another larger gift that Dad left behind. As my brothers and I stood in that nearly empty house, accepting the reality that there was no book, there was no conversation about what would have been in that book. It never crossed my mind to figure out my position relative to my brothers by finding out what each of us "owed" the estate. I suspect that the same was true for my brothers. It never occurred to us to engage in the type of calculation that Dad had sworn off. Without reflection, without discussion, we simply accepted our father's act of forgiveness.

I credit the way our parents brought us up. Which was the biggest gift of all.

Honoring Time

I've got an hour to kill.
[gasp!] Did I just say that?
Killing time?
Time . . . our great gift

Sometimes we say
we have free time.
All time comes free
till we mess with it.

We look for time, find time,
save time, share time.
We spend a lot of time.
We say we make time.
(I don't think so.)

How can we pay homage
to this great gift?
Avoid wasting time?
Use time in an honorable way . . .
serving Life's Work & Life's Play?
Or, just maybe, time uses us.
What about not investing "my" time,
but investing myself *in* time?

Not so much using time for my projects
as serving time's purposes,
the purposes we find
as we open the package
that time delivers to our doorstep
each morning.

Time presents itself to us
continuously, on its own terms.
Maybe investing ourselves in each moment
is a way to show gratitude
for this gift of life.

Time gives us the opportunity
to become ourselves.
We are always becoming
We never complete our becoming.
Time just runs out on us.

"We've already covered that." I cannot count the number of times I've heard that response to a sincere question or an earnest suggestion—in a classroom or a meeting or a conversation.

We have already covered that . . . and "covered" is exactly what the speaker means. Not "addressed" or "considered" or "discussed." Rather: that this idea or concern or thought is covered—meaning that it has been placed out of sight, buried, not to be dug up again.

In those instances, it seems that the purpose of the class or meeting is to cover things. Stop those discussions. It's all settled. There's nothing here to see.

I've been the target of the we've-covered-that weapon, and I can tell you that it is a downer of all kinds: put down, shut down, shot down.

I would like to see more classes and meetings and conversations where topics and problems are "uncovered" and "recovered." Where the thoughts and concerns and values of the participants are revisited. Where those subjects are laid open, primed and ready for us to revisit them

    —to be more widely discussed

    —to be more carefully considered

    —to be re-examined for value missed the last time around

    —to be more deeply understood

Such classes and meetings could be continuing acts of discovery that open minds and mouths and ears, rather than closing them. A never-ceasing inquiry in which there are

—no sacred cows

—no closed questions

—no settled truths

Where the goal is not to check all the boxes and close the book forever, but to stir a curiosity that seeks new encounters with the coming of each opportunity.

So, what would life look like if we stopped covering things? We might have a world in which:

> More conversations could be occasions for learning rather than lecturing
>
> We could spend more time discovering truth and less time declaring it
>
> Authenticity could be prized; conformity, not so much
>
> Political leaders could be allowed to rethink their responses to the problems of an ever-changing world, without being castigated as flip-floppers
>
> Teachers could abandon using the same notes in the classroom year after year
>
> Bosses and parents could find better words than "my way or the highway"
>
> Churches could view revelation as an ongoing process instead of a closed book
>
> We could all strive more to understand, as well as to be understood

In such a world, conversations would be community-building events. Discussions would be valued for themselves, not for their conformity to pre-determined outcomes. All participants would feel invited, encouraged to join in, and would be heard.

Blessed are the peacemakers, we are told. One way to make peace is to listen—conveying our belief that what others have to say is worthy of our consideration, creating together an exploration instead of competing for the last word.

Singing In The Brain

Hiking trails are graded on scales such as Easy/Moderate/Difficult. Easy trails are those that are relatively flat and relatively smooth, with few stones cluttering the way. On such a path, it is easy to fall into a regular gait, walking at a consistent pace. The steady strides call to mind the work of metronomes or drill sergeants.

When walking on an easy trail, I have frequently noticed that I am, unconsciously, playing a song in my mind. A sizeable number of songs are in my subconscious juke box. Typically, when I tune into a song, it is already in progress. With so many songs in my brain's hit parade, I wonder how my mind makes its choice. When I become conscious of a performance in process, it seems that my body has already organized things; each beat of the song is already in time with my heel hitting the ground on each step.

This doesn't happen on a difficult trail. There are too many obstacles to establish a constant pace: stretches that go almost straight up (or down, depending on your direction), stones and large roots that require careful placing of the next step, water to be crossed, piles of boulders demanding the use of a hand or two. I don't recall tuning into a song in mid-play on these kinds of trails—I'm guessing because there is no sustained beat.

As it is on the trail, so it is in the rest of life. In life and on the trail, there are the easy stretches, when it's easy to keep the rhythm, to step in time—smooth sailing. Then there are the difficult patches. There are stops and starts and missteps and puzzles—the times when our focus is down on where each step goes, hesitation when we are unsure about which way to go. Sometimes we look for help in making forward progress, help that can come from others.

I recall one time on an especially difficult path when there was no cadence cluing my brain to strike up a tune. So, I sent an order to my brain for a song and I completed the last portion of that climb, reaching Royal Arch with the assistance of Tom Petty's "I Won't Back Down"—a very un-rhythmical version playing in my head.

By the way: I need to be concerned not only about *what* I do but also *how* I do it. Tom Petty helped me reach the end of that trail, but he did not alert me to the danger of dehydration under a Boulder, Colorado, August afternoon sun . . . as became evident when I passed out an hour after the climb. Ian came to my rescue. Often, I do get by with some help from my friends.

A First Step

"G__ damn it!" he hollered as my car rolled past him. Through my rolled-down window, I then heard him scream "F___ it." At the time, I thought he was responding to some very bad news—he was alone but wearing earbuds.

Moments later, my car and I had come to a stop at the red light, and the pedestrian was passing us on the sidewalk and continuing his profane rant. This time around though, it appeared that he was not engaged in conversation but was shouting into the universe.

The cause of his stream of invectives was now clear: the light had turned red. The timer on the light had assaulted him, interfering with his brisk walk. Pausing only momentarily, he plunged into the intersection, navigating through drivers who were acting on the belief that their green light meant they could Go. Our yeller did reach the other side, thanks to the kindness of a couple of those strangers.

As I watched, I wondered if this man was a powerful figure who was in charge of other people when he wore his work clothes. After all, he did seem to fill the old-fashioned bill: white, male, vigorous, beginning to gray. How ironic, I thought, that this man who was incapable of controlling himself might be in a position of controlling others.

I mused further: what kind of leader could a man be who is so lacking in self-control? This brief incident reminded me of the flight attendants' talks about when the pilot lands the plane on a body of water; you find your own life jacket first and put it on before you help others put theirs on. If this guy is thrown into a rage by a failure to control the timing of traffic signals, then how might he handle other disappointments?

Even more musing: am I jumping to an unfair conclusion, judging him with very little evidence? I could give this man the benefit of the doubt and still reach a generalized concern. If such unproductive responses lurk so near to a person's surface, I wonder about trusting him with the well-being of others. As a good first step when assessing leadership material, I'm leaning toward those who can respond appropriately to their own setbacks, before they are allowed to handle the challenges of others.

A Few Words To Live By

Charlie was a successful lawyer and a highly regarded civic leader. When I read his obituary, my thoughts ran quickly to the advice he had given to others. He delivered his advice, on multiple occasions, to classes of law students who were assembled on graduation day. His comments on professionalism and a legal career during the commencement program were sound . . . but not, I think, as compelling as his closing words:

"Take time to dance with your darlings."

Music: The Great Conjurer

What could possibly be said,
that hasn't already been said,
about the Music?
Music moves us in ways
that pass understanding,
(at least my understanding).
The music speaks
in her own tongue,
taking over our bodies.
Toes tapping, heads nodding,
hands clapping, bodies swaying.
All shook up.

And she takes us out of our bodies,
sending us back to our past,
flying us to the future,
carving out places right there
in the middle of humdrum life,
transporting us to
play, elation, delight.
Transcendence.

The music speaks,
triggering joy, delivering voice,
stirring belief, accompanying grief,
summoning courage, exploring edges,
invoking imagination, jump-starting recollection.

She lifts the tyranny of duty from our shoulders,
she peeks through the clouds of worry,
serves as an antidote to fear, weariness, boredom, and malaise.

The music makes us stronger, bolder, more tender,
illuminates truth, amplifies messages,
uncovers the depth of what we see,
arouses our consciences.

From the top of my head to the core of my being:
Strengthens the heart,
Captures the mind,
Awakens my soul.

A Difference

A good friend once reminded me
of the time when I said,
during a particularly rough patch,
that I believed in
Happy Endings.

I remember saying that.
And believing it.
Upon further reflection,
I think I don't believe
so much in happy endings
(although I have seen some)
as I do believe in
New Beginnings.

They are related,
Endings and Beginnings,
But there is a difference.

Passing Strangers

We were walking downhill on a fairly narrow stretch of the Red Trail in Warner Park, when we encountered a hiker coming our way. Celeste stepped to the side, and as he passed he said, "Thanks, ma'am." I got the same treatment, "Thank you, sir," when he passed by me.

"Ma'am?" "Sir?" My first thought was to wonder if there was something wrong with his eyesight. His hair was as grey as ours. My second thought, though, was that he is kind of like me—at least in this one respect.

I can remember the trip to Seattle, to a large family gathering, when my parents helped me with Ma'ams and Sirs, hoping that my grandmother and aunts and uncles would think I was respecting my elders. Those lessons stuck and those manners sometimes surface as a reflex in all sorts of circumstances.

With more intentionality, I use polite speech with those who serve me—across a counter, over a phone, through a car window, in a line. I want to convey respect for them and appreciation for what they do. The goal is to avoid a superficial thoughtfulness, a fake civility.

Usually, I end one of these interactions with something like "I hope you have a good day." Sometimes, they beat me to the punch, wishing a good day for me first. "You too," is often the reply as I and others have finished the transaction and are ready to move on to the next item on the to-do list. "You too," feels abrupt. When I am on my game, when I am mindful of trying to avoid fake civility, I briefly delay the departure and reply with eight words rather than two: "I hope you have a good day too."

I don't want to be that guy who says a few cheap words to show what a good guy he is. I really do hope that my gesture is occasionally appreciated. (That hope was fanned recently when a person I'd dealt with regularly for a couple of weeks offered, "Thank you for being nice.")

I know that in the grand scheme of things this is still a superficial encounter. I understand that those extra six words may not change that person's day, and certainly not her life. It does make a difference for me, though, to briefly acknowledge that I've been interacting with another person and not with an ATM machine. Who knows? Over time a stranger just might become a neighbor.

One last thought: I looked up "ma'am" on my computer. Google Dictionary gave me three definitions, two of which were under the label "BRITISH." The only other definition it provided—and I kid you not—was under the label "ARCHAIC – NORTH AMERICAN."

I really don't know what to say about that.

ANIMAL SPIRITS

My daughter Susannah gave me a t-shirt that occasionally draws remarks from passersby—like the fellow in the park who hollered as I passed by, "Hey, you've got a squirrel on your shirt with a drink." "Yes, I do," I shouted over my shoulder as I moved along up the trail.

He was right; more precisely it is a squirrel holding up a martini glass with an acorn (in place of an olive) sporting a toothpick.

The shirt has a caption: "Animal Spirits." "Animal spirits" is the term economist John Maynard Keynes used to identify the instincts, proclivities, and emotions that affect decisions we make. While some economic models operate with the proposition that individuals are rational actors, Keynes opened the door for including these "irrational" factors when trying to understand and to project how people actually make choices.

I think it makes sense to include the reality of these kinds of factors when anticipating the responses of others (as well as when making economic policy). Whether these animal spirits should or should not play a role in our decision-making does not interest me. I am accepting the power of emotions and sentiments as facts of life. From time to time, I do encounter decisions made by others that strike me as illogical. I can disagree, but I shouldn't be surprised.

That's the way things are.

Oxymorons?

civil war
typical woman
junk tree
perfect knowledge
almost pregnant
predictable future
bad baby
worthless dreaming
self-interested compassion
self-made man
quick understanding
ugly flower
half truth
permanent solution
calculated mercy
the last weed
bullet-proof plan
justified meanness
wasted goodwill
conditional love

MAS O MENOS

I remember many things my dad said when I was growing up. Things like, "It's a poor carpenter who cusses his tools." On occasions when he let me drive the family car, he would invariably remind me, "Remember, that's transportation, not a toy." Perhaps most often, I recall his short tagline, "Mas o menos."

More or less . . . added as a benediction of sorts . . . signaling that he was close enough. He was a big fan of back-of-the-envelope estimating. He was also a great storyteller. In both of these undertakings, his "mas o menos" declared that he was not interested in a hypersensitive pursuit of details.

Occasionally, as often happens when sons get older, he was "corrected" on a number or a small detail in a story he was telling. He never argued the point. His reply would be a question, something in the vein of "You aren't going to make me a liar over three inches, are you?"—always delivered with a playful gleam in his eye.

This seemingly lackadaisical approach did not reflect a lack of interest in precision in all things. After all, this was the man who could be exact enough in his work to add four rooms and a garage to our house. He was certainly not too lazy to do the work of nailing down precise details. Rather, his mas-o-menos proclamations were indications that he sat easy in the saddle of life.

He kept things in perspective. He majored in big pictures, not trivia, and was not inclined to spend unnecessary time and energy on the small stuff. I admire that matured temperament. Life brings enough struggles our way without us needlessly adding to the pile.

I'm not saying that this gentle type of response to the world is appropriate in every circumstance—just that it is great to have the "It's all small stuff" response in our tool kit.

Both, Please

I participated in an honors program on my way to receiving my B.A. degree from Baylor University. One requirement of that program was to write a substantial research paper during the senior year. It felt like mine ran about 500 pages, but I suspect 40 is closer to the truth. The topic I chose was Obscenity and Profanity. (Hey, that was 1968.)

Before graduation, students had to pass a "defense," meaning we had to answer questions about our papers. In my case, they called in a faculty member from Trinity University to grill me. (Maybe no faculty members at Baylor thought they were well-versed in that subject.) At one point in our session, the visiting professor asked me if obscene language influenced behavior or if the behavior influenced the language.

I was stumped, flustered, calling to mind examples of each possibility. I finally gave up . . . I don't know, I said. The visitor said he thought it was both. I was embarrassed that I had missed something so obvious. I learned a lot that day. Ever since, when facing a problem where "both" is a possible answer, I tend to go with "both."

Fast forward two decades: I was teaching a Bioethics and the Law class at Vanderbilt Law School. When a new Medical Ethics professor came to the Medical School, he and I co-taught that course every year for about a dozen years. He was the guy who came from Trinity to torture me. In this reunion, Richard and I had a great time together.

Our course enrolled equal numbers of law students and medical students. We paired them up, one student from each school, and then we assigned two of the mixed pairs to present, in class, the opposite sides of one of the hypotheticals we had prepared.

The students were not allowed to pick "both" until after they had finished presenting the best argument in favor of their assigned answer. Once their presentations were completed, in the discussion that followed we heard a lot of "it depends."

At first glance, opting for "both" may look like a cop out, a failure to pursue a rigorous examination that would yield the correct answer. In many cases, however, the preference for both is the opposite of a cop out. Such a preference may well be a rejection of over-simplified views of our complex world.

Should I tell the story that is true or the story that leads to more good on this Earth? Should our government preserve liberty or serve justice? Is my role in our community to speak my piece or to listen to others speak theirs? Both, please.

And Then What?

When Gay and I had three teenage children and a fourth not far behind, it was not surprising that we went to see a counselor. It would be fair to say that some of our family's activities were playing out differently than what we parents would have choreographed. We were looking for a third perspective, and we got more than we paid for.

When we had settled into the counselor's office, she asked why we had come. Gay and I described one of the potential scenarios that were keeping us awake at night, one in which one of our children could make some bad choices that would result in a parade of horribles. Once we had finished the description of our nightmare, the counselor asked, "And then what?"

Clearly, she did not understand the threats posed by this potential disaster. We responded with embellishments, more details, another possible calamity. And then she asked, "And then what?"

It may have been about the third "and-then-what" when the light came on for me. She was not interested in hearing about more damages that we could imagine. Nor was she minimizing the seriousness of the outcomes we were dreaming up.

The message I was hearing was this: no matter how awful the behavior, life will go on. Even after the darkest night, the sun will come up the next morning. With the realization that we were not facing the end of life as we knew it, our stress level dropped. As parents, some of our focus could move from desperate efforts to prohibit future actions, to being ready to cope constructively when those things did happen.

The neat thing about this is that (1) I *cannot* control the future, no matter how hard I try, and (2) I *can* control my responses when the future shows up. This reminder allowed us to move from the impossible task of controlling the future to the manageable job of figuring out where we go from here, when pieces of the future become part of the present.

Here is the part about us getting more than we paid for: since the day of that counseling session, I have tried to practice asking, "And then what?" in all facets of my life. Some days I do better than others. It does seem that the more I have practiced this self-interrogation, the less often I borrow problems from the future. That leaves me with more time to live in the present.

42

Some days I listen to the news, even watch it on TV. A healthy democracy depends on the dissemination of valid, pertinent information. I want to be a good citizen. I want to be able to differentiate news from entertainment and to know fake news when I see it. I want to make good decisions. Decisions about voting, letter writing, petitions, donations, and other community activities. When I have made a decision, I want to be able to defend my choice. I might want to try to convince someone else to make the same decision. I want to be known as a well-informed fellow and a lively contributor to conversations . . . especially if there is someone in the conversation who needs to be "set right."

Other days, I'd rather just listen to the Beatles sing "Come Together."

BARRIERS

43

Concrete . . . separates us from the earth that birthed us

Covers . . . skew judgments about books, and about people

Labels . . . create "others"

"Everyone knows" . . . stifles creativity

Clocks . . . turn nature's rhythm into hurry up

Screens and keystrokes . . . replace organic communication

Tribes . . . emphasize "us" and "them"

Money . . . generates self-serving incentives

Dogma . . . claims the only version of truth

Tradition . . . sets suspect habits in concrete

What others think . . . snuffs out dreams

Fear . . . shuts us down

The biggest barrier: Hate

The Letter G

I was the driver and my young daughter was the passenger when she said, "I know what the most important letter in the alphabet is."

"What is it?" I asked.

"G"

"And why is G the most important letter?"

"Because if there was no G, there wouldn't be a God."

I was pleased that she, at her young age, was showing an intellectual curiosity by making that kind of connection. I also hoped that as she got older, she would understand the difference between the signs humans invent and the things toward which the signs point.

I expected that the older version of her would understand that an arrangement of three letters in a particular language is not a deity, that a flag is not the republic for which it stands, and that a beautiful wedding ring is not a good marriage.

She is all grown up now, and she does understand.

Life Goals

My mind was blank. A young friend had just finished college and had called to ask a question: "Other than vocational goals, what were your goals when you graduated from college? What did you want to become?"

The first search of my memory bank turned up nothing. I wanted to contribute more than just saying that I had never set goals of that sort. We agreed to convene on my back porch when we were both back in Nashville. In the meantime, I revisited those long-ago years, looking for examples that might be of some help to him.

His request came with the exclusion of vocational goals, which was just as well. My plan was to teach ethics at the college level. Five jobs, a spell drawing unemployment, and ten years later, I began teaching. I did eventually get to teach ethics for thirty years, but the circuitous route, full of serendipity, looks nothing like a plan.

I turned my thoughts to the non-vocational parts of my life. I attempted to put myself back into my state of mind when I was a recent college graduate. How had I planned for my future? I dove into various aspects of my adulthood: residential location, recreation and entertainment preferences, community involvement, religious communities, my band of friends, avocational pursuits, charitable activities, and the wild and wonderful collection of people who constitute my family.

I will spare you, dear reader, of a presentation of tedious and unimportant details. If there had been any goal setting, it was inconsequential. During my 50+ years as a grownup, each aspect of my life has been shaped by (you can see it coming) circuitous routes and serendipitous happenings. I wouldn't have had it any other way.

I realized that I've benefited from a stream of unexpected opportunities. I am thankful that I did not stick to a dogged pursuit of some master plan. I am grateful for my impromptu responses and my improvised life that those choices created. At the end of my search for the goals that had formed my life, I was ready to talk to my young friend about the importance of being nimble and agile, and the potential of an unscripted life.

Thankful for Something

"It's always something." I can still hear that phrase in the voice of comic genius Gilda Radner. Her playfulness shines through when it is quoted by my Boomer friends.

However, I have also heard "It's always something," in voices that reflect genuine frustration and irritation—like it was a bad thing.

It *is* always something. Perhaps the source of the outsized frustrations and irritations is an unrealistic expectation of perpetual smooth sailing and an uncomplicated life. "Somethings" *will* be with us always . . . like them or not.

What if there wasn't always something?

I've heard that some sharks must keep swimming. If they are not moving forward, they can't breathe by taking oxygen from water moving through their gills. For them, it's always that swimming something, or they die.

It's the same for us . . . except for the swimming part.

"Somethings" come with life. Some will be more welcomed than others, but all of them are a part of living a full life. I can try to wish them away, but wishing won't get the job done. Things *will* be with me as long as I am on this side of death. So, maybe one more thing is not such a bad thing after all.

Different Tunes

I.
"Let It Be," they sing to me,
Some things are beyond your control.
We're not in charge of what life brings,
Not all that's mine will be gold.

Give thanks, they say, for all that is good,
While accepting all the rest.
Live in the mystery of the unknown
And know what you can't possess.

II.
Together we sing "We Will Overcome"
We can't be friends with hate.
We're called to fight till we make things right.
We won't give in to fate.

Give thanks, they say, for all that is good,
But on laurels we cannot rest.
Live through the struggle, win when you can,
And know what you can't possess.

III.
Two good songs.
Two different messages.
Different tunes for different days?

Seen

Look around, now.
Look again, more intently and deeply.
Fully present in the present,
This time and this place
want to show us something.

LABYRINTH

The labyrinth surprised me. As I walked up the main entrance to the Basilica of St. Francis of Assisi in Santa Fe, I glanced to my left and saw it. Unexpected . . . I did not recall it from my visit to that same site ten years earlier. It is massive: 45 feet across, composed of granite blocks of various sizes, shapes, and colors. One question came immediately to mind: do I walk it?

I do not have a long history with labyrinths. I had walked my first one only seven years earlier, when Becca Stevens coaxed me into traveling the one at Dubose Conference Center. Since then, I had walked a labyrinth only a few times. I was self-conscious at the front door of the basilica. No one was walking that labyrinth. Although the plaza was full of people, no one was even looking at it. I imagined that they would all stare at an odd fellow tracing the route, but I started anyway.

Along the way, I noticed that I was walking with my head down, never once looking more than one stone block ahead of my feet. I surmised that I was not wanting to glimpse the gaze of any observers, gazes which might imply their judgments about my trek and would interrupt my thoughts. This head-down approach was a new labyrinth practice for me—in the past, I had looked up, surveying the overall pattern, knowing what was coming and when.

Thus, a new experience was in store for me: I was surprised when I reached the center. At that moment I recalled the time when I had counseled "Trust the Path" to a four-year-old Gilbert. He was walking the labyrinth in the St. Augustine's chapel and he became concerned, even agitated, when his steps seemed to be taking him farther and farther from his goal. "Trust the path," I said to myself in Santa Fe, meditating briefly on the fact that one step at a time is all we ever get.

I then faced another question: do I make the return trip? I hesitated, and then took the first step of the return journey as the cathedral bells marked half past the hour. On the first half of the trip, I had easily maintained a slow, deliberate, unhurried pace, but now I noticed that I was tempted to walk faster. Instinctively my body seemed ready to get it over with. So, I slowed down each time I felt a hurried step, sometimes to an even slower pace than before. Some thoughts came to mind that I wanted to remember—should I finish up quickly and make some notes? Maybe even abandon the rest of the trip? But I stayed with the path.

And then I was surprised again. On the return trip, I was rewarded with a flower, a beautiful single blossom hanging over the outer edge of the labyrinth. I had been at this point minutes before, but the flower had been facing away from me then, and so I had passed it unseeing, unnoticing, when I made the first half of the walk. Now, I took a picture, and moved on.

I reached a point where I noticed a large shadow falling across my path. I stopped. The shadow that was covering the path was the shadow of the cathedral. That building was blocking the sun. Reflecting on my long struggle with the institutional church, I turned my thoughts to how appropriate it was that the darkness covering the path was caused by the church, the institution that often makes it difficult for me to see the true path. A bit self-satisfied with having connected this insight to my walk, I went on.

Almost immediately, I noticed another shadow, one that was even more distracting than that of the cathedral. This shadow was moving, in and out, over and off the path as I moved along, an even larger obstacle to a clear focus on my way forward. It was my own shadow. It was my shadow that was obstructing the view; it was me, my very self, that was interfering with a clear view of the path. As I pondered this unexpected turn in my reflections, I could only smile, nod my head, and say to myself, "Of course."

Of course. Of course, *I* am the main impediment to knowing what I should know and doing what I should do. I don't have perfect knowledge, and what I do know is built on shifting sands—colored by my personal perspectives, my self-interest, my biases and prejudices, my location in the world. This is, of course, the human condition. None of us can escape this reality. The appropriate response is humility.

When I speak, I should do so humbly, knowing how little I really know. When I act, I should do so humbly, knowing that the foundations upon which my actions are built are fragmentary, fluid, and contested.

It is all too easy to forget about these clay feet of mine. I am grateful for that moment in the labyrinth in Santa Fe. It reminds me of who I am, and what I am not.

Dead End Signs

I know what a "Dead End" sign means, but it strikes me that the wording is a bit off base. The sign doesn't really signal an end. When I have proceeded past a dead end sign, I've stopped (temporarily), looked around, and assessed my options; and then, usually, I have turned around and moved on to an alternative path.

So, it is not so much an end as it is an occasion to re-direct my travel in a new direction.

And the "dead" part? Often in my travels, as well as in other aspects of my life, I have been more alive after I have made a change in direction, finding new life elsewhere. Maybe it is the lettering that bothers me. Maybe we could change the wording on the sign to "Turnaround Ahead."

Of course, these thoughts about the wording reflect only my experience. There are millions of people who wake up every morning feeling, for good reason, that they are at a dead end. And they don't need a sign to tell them.

1125.81

Naturally, I should have seen it coming.
My self-congratulatory self,
accompanied by my smug self,
had often proclaimed:
I don't take any medicines,
I don't have any aches or pains,
no dizziness or leakage or limits.

Then there was that test.
This test came with a chart of result numbers:
11-100: risk modification recommended
101-400: aggressive risk modification
1125.81: my score with warnings about
artery disease & cardiovascular events.

Do tests ever lie?
How often are they mistaken?
Could this be a technical artifact?
What about all those appearances
of being in excellent health?
What about that "You'll live
another thirty years" my doctor said—
only three years earlier?
Nevertheless:

That Test Result Day may have been
My First Day of feeling, really feeling,
that I, too, am aging,
the mortal kind of aging.
Naturally.

55

A Night In India

Late one night, I was sharing a hotel bed with Celeste, my wife of twenty years and counting. We were in the middle of an eighteen-day trip to India (my first time in that country). I was wide awake. Celeste was just the opposite . . . sound asleep. I was restless but did not want to wake her. So, I had no option, not even turning on a light to read, except to lie there.

In the past, I had dabbled a little with mindful meditation, but never with much success. With lots of time on my hands, I decided to give it a try. I relaxed, lying still on my back, eyes closed, taking in longer-than-usual breaths, counting slowly as I tried to clear my mind. I was also hoping that this practice might bring on the elusive sleep.

I cannot adequately describe what happened next. I experienced leaving the earth. I was moving farther and farther from our globe. I passed through our solar system and continued past all sorts of celestial bodies, one grouping after another. After an extensive trip, the motion reversed and I was slowly moving back to my starting point. When I got back to Earth, and then to my body, the movement continued. I went into my body, deeper into my body, past organs and through places that I can only label as the molecular level and then the atomic level, the subatomic, and beyond, to whatever is smaller and smaller. Eventually the experience ended with a slow return voyage back to the surface.

I was refreshed. Although I had lost much of a night's sleep, I felt rested. I felt connected to the cosmos—a profound sense that "I" am a part of the universes, and they are in me, in ways I could never understand. I was aware that what I can see with my eyes and hear with my ears are not reliable guides to fully comprehending all that is around me. That same awareness of inadequacy also applies to what I think with my brain.

On one hand, I cannot in any way account for the trip I took that night. On the other hand, in retrospect, I can see how I might have been primed for this late-night voyage. I had done some reading in preparation for the trip to India, but I don't think that was what launched me on that late-night voyage. I believe it was the first-hand experience of India that set the stage for the once in a lifetime journey. Daily, we were visiting Indian spiritual, cultural, and historical sites. We regularly participated in festivals and celebrations with our Indian hosts. I was privileged to converse at some length with Nalin Nirula, a gifted Reiki physician-healer and author. All of this was mind-opening, introducing me to an unfamiliar culture and new perspectives. Every day played host to a compare-and-contrast exercise as I worked to understand the new world I was seeing.

There is no substitute for my Indian experience. Travel can introduce us to new realities, different perspectives, and expose us to other ways of thinking. Travel gets us out of some of our routines and ruts.

 It is also true, however, that it is not necessary to go to another country for two weeks to find novel situations that raise new questions. I can get off my beaten paths with an afternoon in another part of town, an immersion in a remote natural wonderland, or switching to public transportation. Minds can also travel by reading a book, visiting a gallery, or attending a concert . . . even having a conversation.

Habits can shrink my world. Habits may make my life more comfortable and may increase my efficiency in getting along in life.

But at what cost? Sticking to my established habits reduces those occasions when I might investigate my world and fashion new responses to that world. When that happens, I miss opportunities to live a fuller, richer life.

Touching

We touch, from beginning to end, in our life with each other.

In the First Welcome, babies lie on breasts and are held in arms. In subsequent welcomings, we find warm embraces, awkward hugs and hearty hugs, firm handshakes. All kinds of handshakes: polite ones, wholehearted ones, secret ones, and those that are well-choreographed for public display. We suffer when we are deprived of opportunities to touch.

Words of welcome are good. Exchanged glances can be meaningful. But touching is the most intimate, most affirming form of connecting.

In departings, you can find the touching that neither of you wants to end—the movement in a slow, gradual drawn-out ending of the hand-to-hand holding, down to the last finger-to-finger touching until the moment arrives when the last connection gives way to space. That first gap of just a millimeter grows to become inches, feet, yards, miles, sometimes days or years, or the permanence of forever.

We do have other senses:
We can delight in the familiar smell of one another.
We can taste through a sweet kiss.
We can speak the words of caring, concern, sharing.
Through our eyes we can signal and receive signals.
"That touched me," we say, when these other senses move us in meaningful ways.

Without taste or sight or hearing or speaking or smelling, we can still communicate our togetherness, our common love, and our shared hopes . . . we can still connect through bodily contact.

There are, of course, those who abuse the privilege of touching.
The anti-touching.
The slapping, hitting, raping that is the perversion of touching, the abusive touching that creates the opposite of community and communion.
Touching abused is a powerful destructor of persons.

Touching done well is a powerful connector between persons. The essence of touching is mutuality—each touch is given and received in the same moment.

There is also the after-touching. When feeling is gone, when touching is one-sided, when one person's bodily being becomes unable to receive, unable to give the gift of touching, when the body is cold, unfeeling, and dead. The Last Departure: final, total separation.

We know that time will come when all physical connection is broken. Until then we have life, and we know we can share life. Through touching we do share life.

So, while I still can, I will:

Cherish Each Connection
Reach Out
Open My Arms
Extend my Hand
Embrace Others

Stay in Touch

Pass It On

She was about eight years old, in the Ecuadorian village I was visiting on a medical mission trip for the seventh time. The children had performed a dance program out on the concrete slab that was most often used as a soccer field. A downpour cut short the program that evening. I had moved into the relatively dry sanctuary, sitting on the floor in my plastic poncho. She came in the open doorway, looked around, and then headed straight for me. Through her gestures and those smiling eyes, she let me know that she wanted me to give her the poncho.

I did, willingly, feeling good that that $2 piece of plastic would make her trek home that night a little drier. I felt even better as I watched her return to the doorway and slip the poncho over a four-year-old brother, covering him for the rain-soaked journey home.

Passing it on.

In another kind of village, my eighteen-year-old son Josh and I emerged from a government building, after I had helped him out of a financial hole. He thanked me again, then asked if I could "loan" him another $20 to get some gas and something to eat. The small bills in my billfold came to almost $20, and I handed them to him. Another thanks, and we parted. I followed his car out of the parking lot.

When we came to the first intersection, the light was red. While he was stopped there, he reached out through the passenger-side window and handed some of those bills to the fellow standing on the corner, holding a cardboard sign. I didn't try to see what was written on the sign. Don't they all say the same? *Pass it on.*

I won the lottery. Not one sponsored by the government (one of those that prey on low-income people to keep taxes low). I won what could be considered a more important lottery. I was born as a white, straight male, experiencing no disabilities, in the United States of America, in the middle of the twentieth century. As luck would have it (and, of course it was luck), this set of random characteristics meant that I started my journey through life facing fewer headwinds than were faced by most of the people living on this planet. Not because of any inherent value possessed by these characteristics, but because of skewed societal perspectives and the current arrangement of power in this world.

The scales were further tipped in my favor because I was born into a loving family, with middle-class parents who would spend the next thirty years doing everything they could to nurture, protect, and support me. I know that I did nothing to deserve these advantages. I also know what I need to do with this inheritance that came my way on Day One: be grateful. And, drawing on the humbling examples of these two children: Pass It On.

The Woman Who Talks To Squirrels

"Move on, now," she calls,
to the squirrel in her path.
And the squirrel obeys.

She twirls among the wind-blown blizzard
of fall leaves, more delighted than if
hundred-dollar bills were showered on her.

She knows no better picture show than
the rolling thunder, flashing lightning, and driving rain
that Nature provides to lift her spirits.

Cartwheeling on a grassy lawn to see that she still can,
after that time she broke her wrist walking backwards
looking upward along a trail among the tall trees.

She sits by running water,
full of sounds and smells and sights,
moving on to what comes next.

Cardinals, wrens, and chickadees
join in her celebration,
along with an occasional owl or hawk.

Among Nature. Where her soul is restored,
where she finds peace and partakes in communion.
Sounds like a church.

When we are in the Inside Church,
her shoulder nudges my arm
each time she hears the hymn begin
"All creatures of our God and King,"

and a little bit of that Great Cathedral
slips past the brick and mortar
and onto our pew.   64

Lessons From A Virus

Before the coronavirus came, I felt bullet-proof. I felt like I possessed a body with extraordinary defenses, one that came with a capacity to heal itself when it was under attack. I often made choices based on that assumption. In fact, I hypothesized that my deliberate careless choices from childhood on might be the source of my strong defenses. (Examples include running in the fog of a mosquito-killing chemical [DDT?] that was spewing out the back of a truck that was driving down our street, refusing to apply sunscreen, using my mouth to hold all sorts of things—such as nails—when I needed a third hand.) In my fantasy world, these practices surely built a strong immune system.

After the coronavirus came, I still felt bullet-proof. But I chose to act on a different feeling.

Elizabeth and Sarah Jordan, my in-town daughters, joined that army of millennials that took it upon themselves to bring awareness to their elders. I was touched by their efforts. The core of their message, at least as I received it, was that my decisions affected folks other than myself. I felt that I should make those few, easy choices that could extend the time I'd be on this earth (and help others avoid the virus as well).

* * * * *

I was sitting on the front porch swing,
watching the sundown clouds float my way.
I was sitting long-ways on the swing,
the chain cutting into my back.
That felt right because

I shouldn't be comfortable when
a good man had just died.

I lit a candle for his wife.
You can tell me that that doesn't do any good.
I can tell you that nothing I could do
will do any good.

Well, that's not quite right.
I did tell Celeste that I loved her.
She said, "You must not get this [virus]."

* * * * *

"I've never seen that before." I found myself making that obser-
vation repeatedly, early in the Covid-19 season. Our daily routine
included a walk, a hike, or bike ride—in parks, on greenways, or
on streets in our part of town. On those outings, I often noticed
things that I had not noticed before. Among the list of notables
were cactus growing in a front yard, a house sited across the river,
a very, very tall oak tree, and metal steps leading up to the railroad
tracks that run through our neighborhood.

What struck me about those sightings is where they all occurred.
I had been at each of those places before, many times—and I had
not been blindfolded on those prior visits.

I expect to see something new in my first visit to a National Park.
I'm also learning to expect to make new discoveries in the parks
and paths and streets closer to home, even if I've been there before.

* * * * *

A view from our front porch:
Children on wheels,
Bikes and Trikes and Big Wheels

Strollers, Skates, Scooters, and Skateboards
With a new message for the cars:
Beware, this is our playground now.

Grownups on foot,
Walkers and Runners
Joggers and Dalliers
Some with a beverage in hand
All of them waving
All of them sending the message:
We're all in this together.

Waving the message:
We are not just a bunch of houses
We are a Neighborhood.

* * * * *

My friend Sam arrived late to a Zoom meeting. He appeared
on my screen about halfway through our session, slouched on a
couch with one of his children in his lap, far from his camera. If he
said anything during the meeting, I did not hear it.

He is a nurse, and he was on the frontlines in one of our city's
major hospitals. Sensing that he was going through a rough patch,
I lit a candle for him. I later learned that he had lost one of his
patients that day. The next week, I sent him a note mentioning
the candle-lighting. He was gracious in his response: "When I was
younger candle lighting for others didn't quite make sense to me.
But now it does, why I'm not sure."

"Why I'm not sure." I could have written that comment. I pon-
dered: could I do any better by candle-lighting? Could I affirm
something more than to say I don't know? The white flag of sur-
render came to mind. Waving that flag accepts the reality at hand

and signals the judgment that additional efforts to change things would be fruitless. Candle-lighting is also an acceptance of a reality—a response to events such as death or other life shattering developments. Did the lighting also convey an understanding that reversing the reality at hand is beyond our power?

I decided I wanted to communicate a different message when I light a candle: I am with you, I am for you, I embrace you and want to travel this road with you. On those occasions when words fail me, the act of lighting a candle offers a good substitute. I have continued to light candles.

* * * * *

My daughter tested positive for Covid-19.
My contact with her put me into a fourteen-day self-isolation.
I had no symptoms; I was sure that I was not infected.
I was tested on the sixth day. I got the results on the eighth.
Negative.
But in those seconds while I was waiting for the result to appear on my screen, I realized that I was *not* sure.

Sometimes the little lies I tell myself serve my purposes. I would not have wanted to live all those eight days with the anxiety that arose during those last few seconds when I was waiting for the news.

ONCE UPON A GAGGLE

For as long as I can remember, "gaggle" has been a delightfully odd word. One morning I came upon a gaggle of geese. Definitely a gaggle.

Maybe two dozen of them. Resting, eating, meandering, fertilizing as only geese can fertilize. I took a picture—two, actually. Before the second shot, I noticed other passersby taking out their cameras . . . validating my sense that this was indeed a gaggle.

I had plenty of time to reflect on their impromptu gathering as I walked on. Perhaps it was not so impromptu. For all I know, they agreed the night before—alright, tomorrow morning, Centennial lawn, before the sun clears the tree line.

My reflection turned to other large groupings. The Purple Martins we witnessed in downtown Nashville, diving into their roost at sunset—hundreds of thousands we were told. Seemingly countless bats, streaming out of their cave before sunset. Homo sapiens congregating at the Lincoln Memorial to hear about a dream. Hundreds of thousands taking to the streets of Hong Kong giving voice to their dreams. Smaller groups: 100,000 filling a stadium to cheer on the players—musicians or athletes—players they had never met, but loved just the same.

There is something about a crowd that draws us together. Not always. Not everyone. But often enough that it's worthwhile to reflect on such behavior. We do want to belong, and in those mass moments we are connected to nameless others through common bonds of purpose and affection.

We not only share that time in time; we create a shared history. Our gaggles generate stories. Over and over in years to come we will ask, "Remember that time when . . . ?" In that storytelling, we will affirm our past, renew what we value, and rejoin our compatriots.

I could hardly wait until I got home that evening to tell my story about the gaggle on the lawn of Centennial Park.

At the Crosswalk

There's this crosswalk that has been a part of my daily life for years. When the white lights form the walking stick figure, I cross the street in the morning heading south. In the afternoon, I make the passage heading north. West End is a busy five-lane thoroughfare. So, on the occasions when I am stopped by the orange lights that create a hand that signals "halt," my wait for the white lights that signal "walk" is often a long one.

For too much of my life, I was a bit aggravated by the time I wasted there. It was not unusual for me to go to some lengths to avoid that waste. I could see the lights from almost a block away. As the intersection drew nearer, if the chances increased that I could make the next light, I would pick up the pace. The closer I got, the more I hurried, rushing to save my time. Occasionally, a change of lights would come so late that they set me off jogging, running the last few steps to avoid the stop. (Over time, I observed many other pedestrians doing the same thing, dashing to the intersection with backpacks bouncing and briefcases swinging.)

During the long wait that came when I was caught by the traffic signal, I would review my prior actions—the ones that had brought my life to this abrupt halt. What if I'd left the car in the parking lot twenty seconds earlier? What if I had picked up the pace sooner? What if I'd driven through that last yellow light on the way to the parking lot?

Eventually, I learned to Stop, or more accurately, to love the Stop. A full stop, not the kind of rolling stop that is practiced at a stop sign on a deserted street, or even the stop when your car inches forward before the light turns green—but a true full stop.

And not just stopping the forward motion, but also being at peace with the stop. Living at that stop, not allowing the mind to run ahead to the destination while the rest of the body has to wait.

I came to view this time as Stop. Breathe. See. Accepting the gift of time that arrives in every moment. An opening of each present.

Living in that now . . . in that place.
Playing the hand that time had dealt me.
A timeout from the morning routine.
Using that time to breathe deeply, slowly, luxuriously.
Using that space, just before the crosswalk, to look around, to take in the sights and sounds that I would have missed had I dashed across those five lanes.
Freeing my mind to rest, or to wander around in that moment and see what I could find.

Stop. Breathe. See. Kind of like the "Stop, Look, and Listen" that we learned in driver's education class. We learned that Stop-Look-Listen could save our lives; that practicing that simple safety habit could extend our lives.

I have come to believe that practicing the Stop-Breathe-See habit could also extend my life. At many other places as well, not just at that crosswalk.

Keeping Up Appearances

I do not recall what brought me to the post office that day. I do, however, have a clear memory of what I saw. Waiting for my turn at the counter, I looked around and was struck by the condition of the room: paper peeling off the walls, an ancient paint job that was dingy and smudged, holes in the walls that appeared to be the former homes for pictures and plaques.

A pile of thoughts tumbled into my mind:

> Did I just not notice this shabbiness on my last visit?
>
> Do they have plans to do something about this soon?
>
> Do these conditions affect staff morale?
>
> Given the reported post office deficits, am I glad that they aren't spending a lot of money on appearances?
>
> Are appearances unimportant for a government operation that runs as a quasi-monopoly?

Days later, one last question was still rolling around in my brain. What do I think about keeping up appearances? Is keeping up appearances a good thing or a bad thing? The answer seems to be: It Depends. It depends on a jumble of motivations, commitments, values, relationships, effects, understandings, expectations, and more.

Judgments based on such considerations allow us to discern the difference between (1) the charades and shams and fakes where outer appearances hide the reality that lies within, and (2) the other kinds of exteriors that truly reflect the inner substance.

My challenge is to avoid taking the easy path that confuses one with the other.

74

Invitations

Blue Sky, Gray Cross, Red Brick.
The steeple invites
all those people on the outside
to come in.

Some of those people on the outside
silently invite the inside people
to come out,
out from under the steeple.

Get Out of the House

Get out of the house,
out the doors.

Shedding the contaminants
from the frenetic world that bears down on us.
Passing among the big trees where the big winds
make the only sound you can hear.
See the sunset, not through the living room window
but on the horizon that reaches farther
than you can reach.
If the clouds that make the spectacular sunsets
have gone AWOL,
turn around, look east, and see the harvest moon
just rising over the outstretched limbs.

Run a bit in the grass. Not because you are in a hurry,
but just because you can.
Find a bluff, and look as far as you can,
then see farther.
Tune your ears to the calls of the birds,
who are announcing your arrival
and bidding you farewell.
Imagine what they look like,
especially when you don't have a clue.
Take note of the creatures who share the earth with us,
even if you can only find a squirrel . . . or an ant.

Push yourself, challenge your body,
knowing that relief is just beyond the crest.
Slow walk the path,

knowing that it's a waltz, not a race.
Stop and sit a spell,
knowing that that's a good posture for taking it all in.
Nature knows how to put on a show.

Lift your eyes,
see the tops of the trees (in the winter)
trace the clouds' journeys.
Lower your gaze,
discover one patch of wildflowers mingling with another
next to sentinel stones quietly standing guard.

Follow the leaves:
Buds coming to life in the spring.
Summer leaves dancing in brilliant sunlight.
Forming an artistic masterpiece with their fall colors.
Covering the winter floor, burying the earth
as it rests before bringing forth life once again.

Play in the water.
The moving water, so many moving waters
giving us a new snapshot every moment:
flows, ripples, waves, rapids, falls.
The still water, bringing us peace and quiet and serenity.
Wiggle your toes in the water, wade in the shallows,
rinse off your hands, splash your hot, dry face.
Why not the whole body?

Maybe there are limits to the out of doors
But I know I'll never find them.

p.s. turn off the cellphone

Her Skin Was So Familiar

Holding her hand in mine,
my mind wandered through the past,
stopping occasionally at cherished times and places.

We had come to visit for a week.
We stayed three weeks.
She spent those weeks in the hospital bed
shoved up against the picture window in the living room.

She did not see the palm trees or the bougainvillea.
All our eyes were on her,
her chest barely rising and falling
with each shallow breath.
The nurse was careful with the morphine doses.
My brothers and I wouldn't have minded more.

One day she roused.
"It hurts," she whispered.
"It will get better," I responded.
She asked, "Because I am going to die?"
"Yes."
Then she uttered the last words I would ever hear from her:
"I've stopped eating. Maybe that will help."

Her skin was so familiar,
as I held my mother's still-warm hand in mine.
Saying goodbye to her,
after she had said her final goodbye.

Loneliness

Loneliness is not aloneness.
We know that.
I have been lonely at a dinner table of twelve,
as a spectator, looking through a transparent wall
at a talkative crowd that had no interest in
what I might have to say.

I've been lonely in a room filled with a hundred people or more,
as an observer of a bunch of strangers
at more than arm's length, putting on a performance
which had no role for me.

The difference between loneliness and aloneness is the difference
Between friends on the one hand, and associates & acquain-
tances on the other
Between belonging to a tribe and living among a lot of people
Between reaching out to others because you know you'll be
welcomed, and
holding back because you aren't sure.

It is the difference between occupying time & space with others,
and engaging them & being engaged by them,
deeply and widely and over time, the more time the better.

Deeply: talking about more than the weather.
Widely: caring about another and caring about what the other
cares about.
Over Time: conversations piling one upon another
until the sedimented history has constructed a foundation
that will hold you up through absence and misunderstanding
and disagreement.

The antidote for loneliness is connection.
Finding a connection can be risky, like daring to
walk on a seemingly frozen pond,
feet creeping out over the edge
testing the surface. Will it hold?
There's only one way to find out,
inch by inch, one foot carefully in front of the other,
looking, listening for signs of cracking.
Moving slowly.
After all, you don't run headlong
to the middle of a maybe-frozen pond.

And it might fail
with feet crashing through the not-quite frozen surface.
If the surface gives way, then what?
It's cold, wet feet. They will dry off and warm up
for another try, later.
But if the venture does not fail,
if you find yourself in new territory,
you will experience a nearly miraculous
walking on water.

Like most things of value, pursuit requires a gamble.
Whether venturing out on the ice,
or venturing to make a new connection.
When the connection holds
life is a bit richer and fuller
with a new relationship
that can carry us through
even when we are alone.

My Watch and Me

I was an avid watch watcher. During the 24 hours allotted for each day, I was almost obsessed about how far along I was on the clock. I was constantly glancing at my watch, often more out of habit than to obtain useful information. At times, a second look was needed for the hours and minutes to register in my mind. On those rare occasions, when the watch was not in place, I would still be glancing at my wrist.

That watch was always with me, of course. I strapped it on while dressing every morning and it was one of the last things off at night. The time came when I wanted to reduce the level of urgency in my life. I thought taking off my watch might help. I was right.

Wearing my watch was no longer an everyday, all-day affair. It became an intentional decision for a few specific occasions. Leaving the watch on my chest of drawers felt akin to a mindfulness breathing exercise. There were, of course, still plenty of other ways to know the time when necessary (see the cell phone).

Life became less urgent. Reducing urgency does not have to mean losing interest in serious issues and problems. I was looking for a difference in *how* to address such problems. I found a different flow to my inner life.

Haste really does make waste. I have found that a less hurried approach:

—prevents a rush to judgment

—fosters reflection, contemplation, clarity

—makes room for conversation with others

—avoids the tyranny of self-imposed deadlines

—eliminates quick responses that lead to mistakes

—reduces unnecessary angst

—creates time for discernment, decreases wasted motion

—feeds the self

Let the Dust Settle

Forrest Gump famously said, "Life is like a box of chocolates." And it's true; often you don't know what you're going to get. The same can be true of a walk to work.

Occasionally, I walk to the chapel where I spend many of my working hours. Recently, on one of these walks, I encountered a large street sweeping machine, which was stirring up all sorts of things before me in the street's gutter. I usually walk briskly (after all, I'm doing this for exercise), but as the morning sun lit up that dust storm, I slowed my pace. Letting the dust settle.

Some minutes later, I had moved off the street and onto a greenway under construction. I rounded a bend that I'd rounded before and confronted an asphalt-laying machine. (Did I mention the greenway was under construction?) What was then called for was not a slowing to let the asphalt settle but something more radical; I abruptly swerved off my course and looked for a new way forward.

Lesson learned, again: adjust my travel to changing circumstances—on a walk, and in life.

We like our routines. We complain about things that disrupt our routines. We talk about wanting to get back into our routines, especially the ones that we have fashioned ourselves. Slavishly following them can shrink our lives.

The dust and the asphalt interrupted my routine walk. They pushed me away from the direction and pace of my usual journey. Similar types of interruptions in life push us out of our settled habits, forcing us out of our run-of-the-mill patterns. Sometimes, life dumps a pile of hot asphalt on our path, right in front of us.

A death in the family. A lost job. Circumstances have already grabbed our attention and demanded a disruption in familiar practices.

What about the times when our routine seems to be serving us well, when the sailing is smooth and the living is easy? Sometimes, I get so comfortable in my routines that I don't notice where I am, appreciate where I have been, or value the opportunities that lie before me. Early in life, our future stretches before us as a broad plain of almost endless possibilities. As time goes by, we make choices. Choosing one option means rejecting and declining other possibilities. Gradually, the wide plain looks more and more like a rutted road—not because there are no longer other opportunities, but because we aren't paying attention as we follow the well-worn path.

When I look around and take stock of new possibilities, I can sometimes see beyond the ruts. I can rouse myself from my complacency. I can move out of a perfectly nice routine, into one that enhances my life and, I hope, the lives of others. It's possible to stir up a whirlwind of prospects and make new choices as I let the dust settle.

My Bicycle

I bought my first new bicycle in years. I also bought a little battery-powered bike computer that I mounted on the handlebars. This accessory could tell me how far I had gone on a ride, down to a hundredth of a mile. It could also tell me how long that ride lasted, down to a tenth of a second. I could use the calculator application on my phone to figure out the miles-per-hour for that ride, down to seven decimal places.

To what end, I didn't know.

When the battery wore out, I replaced it, and the computer came to life again. When the battery wore out the second time, I replaced it again. Eventually, the battery wore out once again.

I had not come up with an answer to the question, "To what end?" So, I did not replace the battery.

Nevertheless, I continue to enjoy, and benefit from, my bike rides.

Stories From the Water

Walk down to the docks
Scan the harbor.
More boats than you can count.

Some are little more than inner tubes with small outboard
motors,
others are floating mansions.
In between are two-masted sailboats, trawlers, and ski boats.

Each one is unique.
Each one has its own story.
Each one is its own story.

It is that time of day when all is quiet, silent, still.
Nothing is moving
except the ducks,
and the mother taking pictures of her children on the shore.
Yet, from that peaceful scene, each boat shouts out its story:

Of the sailor who races every chance she gets
The shrimper whose nets fill the markets
The parents who immerse their children in a wider water
The craftsman who scrimps and saves to build his dream boat
The angler who keeps food on the kitchen table
The traveler seeking new worlds, delighting in distant shores
The host who spreads pleasure before family and friends.
All of them the dreamer who answers the call of that domain
where the footing is never firm.

One harbor: countless boats
Around this planet: countless harbors, even more countless boats

Every one of them resting, together,
on the single body of water that wraps around our globe.

Even in their infinite numbers and geographic remoteness,
each one still has its own story.
Each story is still precious.
Each life is still precious.
Even if the boat
is not resting in my hometown,
even if it is moored in
another state or a foreign land,
Each life is precious.

Thought

Thoughts, values, philosophies,
impressions, beliefs, ideas,
notions, theories, and convictions.
All of these well up inside us as we navigate life's journey.

Thoughts arrive
under their own power
like volunteer plants.
We can shape these guests
through intentional cultivation.

An Ethics Primer

1. Don't Rush to Judgment
   If you think that *all* of the good reasons in any moral argument are on your side, you probably haven't thought enough

2. Use Your Heart and Your Head
   Don't let efficiency rule out compassion
   or vice versa

3. Expect Change and Surprises
   This will foster humility in your words and deeds

4. Accept the Present
   Don't deal in a world you would prefer instead of the one we have

5. Remember, Real People Get Hurt
   Ethics is not a board game

6. Use Your Words
   Good advice for children is imperative for grown-ups

7. Be Aware of the Money
   The pull of greed cannot be overestimated

8. Tell the Truth, to Yourself and to Others
   Because we should

9. Balance Liberty and Justice
   Where you sit affects where you stand when weighing these two

10. Treasure the Common Ground
    It's our common purpose that holds us together

11. Tread Carefully Around Irreversible Decisions
    Some mistakes cannot be corrected

12. Think Again
    Just because you learned something first doesn't make it right
        It doesn't make it wrong, either

13. Protect the Vulnerable
    Who can't protect themselves

14. Reject Foolish Consistency
    Sometimes the ends justify the means
        sometimes they don't

15. Master Saying "I Don't Know"
    Because often we just don't know

16. Take the Long View
    Life is long, history is longer

17. Do Unto Others as You Would Have Them Do Unto You
    Of course

18. Love Without Judgment
    Care about those who have not "earned" it

One Day At A Time

Life is one day at a time
For all of us.
No one gets to live two days
in a 24-hour period.

This day, today, is all we get.
Nobody gets a do-over
for yesterday or last year.
Nobody starts living tomorrow
until today's clock strikes midnight.

So, we are all on the same plane.
We all live one day at a time,
Time is the great leveler—
Except it's not.

A while back, a good friend called, saying his parole had been approved. Another friend asked about my expectations for him, and I said that he would be taking things one day at a time. Then, I started reflecting on what it meant to take life one day at a time.

It means something different for me than it does for my friend. And it means something different for the women in the Magdalene program at Thistle Farms, who I heard speak that same week about their continuing recovery from addiction. And it means something different for a refugee in a camp in war-torn Syria.

Finding this day's bread
while tomorrow's is a mystery
is not the same
as finding today's bread

in a pantry stocked
with a six-month supply.

Getting one more day's work
from the day labor truck
is not the same
as knowing that you will never
have to visit the day labor truck.

Giving thanks at bedtime
that your children
have been safe for one more day
is not the same
as taking their safety
for granted, every day.

There is a difference between
Living day to day
when the leap from one day to the next
is full of fear, worry and uncertainty,
and
Living day to day
when one day smoothly
melds into the next day
as far as the eye can see.

Voices

All the world's a classroom. Each of us is a learner. Our homework is never finished, tests come every day, and there is no vacation in the summer. None of us make straight As.

All the world's a classroom, and each of us is a teacher. Every day, eyes are on us. We send messages through our words and deeds. Actions speak as words, and whether we like it or not, the lives we live are heard.

We do live our lives as voices.

How Is Happiness Doing?

I've been hearing that we are having an epidemic of unhappiness in this country.

Throughout human history, there have been impediments to happiness. Famine, plague, and war would make a top ten list, and these continue to assault way too many people around our globe. I have also been told that many people who are well-fed, relatively healthy and residing outside of war zones are unhappy—maybe increasingly so.

To the extent that this is true, I'm sure there are multiple suspects to blame. Here's one thought:

It seems like one of the roads to unhappiness can be traced to the advent of television. We started seeing people coming into our living rooms who were paid to act like they were happy, selling us the things that made them happy: the cars they drove, the cereal they ate, the beer they drank . . . back then even the cigarettes they smoked (which, of course, wrecked health and shortened lives in the real world).

The message: if we could buy some of those things, then we would be happy too. But there was always a gap between those possibilities and what we could afford. Also, there was a gap between what they promised and what the goods delivered. Furthermore, they were not just showing us how to meet our needs; they were turning a spotlight on needs that we didn't know we had, and even more insidiously creating needs that we did not have. Surely, some of the advertisements undermined the appreciation of the way average Americans lived their daily lives.

What seeped into our lives in that earlier era of TV became a torrent of information that came our way with the advent of the digital connection and "social" media. No longer was the intrusion limited to commercials every ten minutes when the TV was turned on. Today we are constantly surrounded by happy "friends." We are regularly informed through virtual connections about what many others are doing or thinking.

The online Oxford Dictionaries gives us this definition of "virtual": "not physically existing as such, but made by software to appear to do so."

"Made by software to appear" to exist. Friends and others appear on our screens and advertise their lives. This communication can expose the gaps between our lives and the lives that seemingly everyone else advertises about themselves. It's no longer just a few actors being paid to point out our life's shortcomings. Millions of people are displaying their great lives and the great times they are having—without us.

How is happiness doing? Discontent and dissatisfaction flow foreseeably from this new form of advertising. Disappointing comparisons and unrealized expectations are predictable outcomes. It's not surprising if happiness is not doing so well for a growing number of people.

A Word for the Rest of Us

Maybe we need a new word,
A word for the rest of us.
A word that tells us, when we go to bed at night,

Why we are here,
Despite our moral mediocrity.

A word other than the *courage*
of firefighters and nurses who save lives.
Other than the *passion*
of artists and musicians who lift and inspire us.
Other than the stirring *eloquence* of preachers
who help us glimpse transcendence.
Other than the *compassion* of those
who empty themselves to save the rest of us,
as did Gandhi and Jesus and MLK.

Maybe we need a new word
to value the lives of the rest of us.
A word to tell us why we should not despair
at the end of another day of unfulfilled promise.

Or maybe we already have that word,
that word, birthed in grace and mercy,
that word: Forgiven.

The Courage Of My Convictions

What are the odds that I am always right? What are the odds that you are always right? I suspect that it's fairly unlikely that I, or you, or anyone else is going to always be right. Although, I guess for the sake of consistency, I should add, "But I may be wrong about that."

If you were around me and listened carefully to my words over time, you would notice that sometimes I try to avoid absolute pronouncements by using hedge phrases such as:

> As I understand it . . .
>
> It seems to me that . . .
>
> From what I've read . . .
>
> As near as I can tell . . .

You might conclude that I don't have the courage of my convictions, that I don't have confidence in what I'm saying.

I have developed this habit as a way of being honest with myself in two ways. First, I am acknowledging that most of what I know has been passed along to me by others. When I survey what I "know," only a small portion is grounded in my direct personal experience. The rest has come to me through what I've read or heard second-hand, and is therefore subject to challenge.

Second, things change. Time flows constantly, all living things change, including circumstances and opinions. Scientists tell us that even the universe itself is here only for a while. I am an adherent of "For Now." Have you been around when someone admits "I was wrong?" It's a beautiful moment, and a testament to this fundamental aspect of life. Even when I get to a place where my footing is as firm as it could ever be, I still must add (if only in my mind) "*for now.*"

I am willing to label my convictions as Provisional Convictions. These convictions are what I believe, what I aspire to, where I stand . . . provided that some new information or revelation doesn't come along to teach me something new, often through my mistakes.

Provisional Convictions sound weak. It may sound like I lack the courage to embrace absolute convictions. It may appear that my tentative commitments are built on shifting sands and would lead to a social paralysis that fails to provide grounds for action.

I vote based on provisional convictions.
I write letters and donate funds based on these convictions.
I have taught classes and written books, and have volunteered, marched, and protested,
And I have raised children to have the courage of their convictions.

Maybe it takes more courage to act on provisional convictions than it takes for those who have absolute answers and the conviction that they are never wrong.

The Atheist

These thoughts were born in a texting exchange with a stranger.

I didn't intend to text a stranger. Using the number in the contacts list on my phone, I tried to text my friend Jennifer. Here's how the texting exchange played out, **verbatim**:

Me: I'm on my way out to Thistle Farms to return the tables loaned for the River Baptism, and some teacups.

"Jennifer": River baptism? That's really cool, what denomination still does that? This is a wrong number though by the way.

Me: Sorry. I'll delete from my contacts. St. Augustine's Chapel on the Vanderbilt campus does this baptism annually.

"Jennifer": That's really cool and authentic. I'm actually atheist but I appreciate different cultures. Have a great day, and it's no problem :)

Me: Some of my best friends are atheist. :)) Hope you have a great day too.

"Jennifer": That means a lot to me to hear that. You've really made my day.

Me: Some of my friends at St. Augustine's likely fall into the atheist category. Actually there have been days when I do too.

"Jennifer": Well if you ever want to talk about, I'm here. Sometimes it's hard because of our society and families. When I gained the courage to stand up for my nonbelief two of my family members disowned me, it can be hard. Anyway, I'm here if you ever need to talk.

Me: I'd be glad to meet with you, maybe over a cup of coffee . . . or whatever your preferred beverage is. I'm about to leave town for 12 days, but could check back in when I've returned.

[Thirteen days later]

Me: I'm back in town. Would you like to meet? Maybe over a cup of coffee?

[end of verbatim]

* * * * *

I never heard from her again. (For some reason, I had assumed it was a "her" all along. Celeste, when I showed her the texts, assumed it was a "he.") I hope this exchange with my unknown friend brought her a bit of comfort, maybe a little more peace of mind.

I have pondered my comment that there have been days when I fall into the atheist category. What did I mean by that? I consulted my Random House Unabridged Dictionary, which says "atheist" is "one who denies or disbelieves in the existence of God or gods." Well, that does seem to be an overly extreme description of where I've been.

There have been stretches, however, when I have lived my life and have found meaning in life, without reference to the concept of God, or using the word "God." The problem I have with "God" is that if I say I believe in God, it seems like I should be able to say what God is. Should a profession of faith require an ability to describe what I believe in?

When asked about God, I sometimes resort to pointing out that at the beginning of my divinity school education, I was taught that God was "ineffable." Of course, at the Divinity School, after they told us that God could not be described, they spent years telling us how people had described God.

Ineffable. Meaning "incapable of being described" (same dictionary). I do believe in that. I do believe that when folks use the word God, they are referring to something that can't be described. Is that another way of saying that they don't know what they are talking about?

On my religious days, the best profession of faith I can come up with is: God is Love. That's it. That may not seem like a lot, but that's the best I can do. For me, putting all of the meaning of that four-letter word (love) onto that three-letter word (god) *is* a lot. I worry about what happens when people start assigning additional content to the word God, when they start saying something more than "God is Love." That may be when the trouble begins for my atheist friend and many others like her.

The Eye Of The Beholder?

In 2020, I began to walk more. In the park, on the greenways, to town, in our neighborhood. Our neighborhood streets wind through a residential area, and we walk *in* those streets because there are no sidewalks. Unfortunately, we have to share those streets with a significant number of trucks and cars that cut through our otherwise peaceful community.

I walk on the side of the street where I am facing the oncoming traffic. As each vehicle approaches, I raise my right hand, about even with my face, palm facing the oncoming driver, fingers extended, sometimes with a slight wave. I've imagined that different drivers infer different messages being sent by my hand. Messages such as:

> "Thank you for driving slowly."
>
> "Slow down, you jerk."
>
> "Howdy, neighbor!"

We know that different people often have varying responses when they see the same thing. We've been told that we can account for this by understanding that it's all in the eye of the beholder. I think that sometimes it's all in the heart of the beholder.

Often, we see what we are prepared to see. If I am speeding through a residential area, I might expect a resident to chastise me and I will interpret what I see in that context. What we are supposing, what we are presuming as we enter a situation, has a lot to do with how we interpret what we see in that situation.

If our hearts are set on expecting good, we're more likely to see good. If they are set on expecting bad, we're more likely to find bad. It seems to me that there are good reasons to set our hearts on good as often as we can.

TAKING OFF

Tray tables stowed, seats in the upright position.
A final look at the trail map, then heading out.
One last push, and one person becomes two.

Preparing for take offs all of our lives,
from beginning to end, often with helpers:
flight attendants, trail guides, midwives.

Breaking away from the status quo,
leaving the ordinary,
moving out of the routine
into the unknown.
Only uncertainty is certain.
That's why we take off, for the novelty.

Do we over-prepare?
Locking in details
to prevent surprise,
to manage the future,
to control the uncontrollable?

Can we
avoid being bound by predictions and forecasts,
leave room for magic,
let ourselves be amazed,
and transform our failures into experiments?

 Every day offers us opportunity
for a new discovery.
In an unprepared moment
we might catch a glimpse of one.

RE-WORDS

We all know what it is like to *re*-something. You know, like to *re*visit or to *re*consider. Take a look at this list:

review

re-examine

reassess

rethink

re-evaluate

reappraise

recheck

reweigh

rehash

These words identify an opening of our minds.

I have noticed that some of us have a greater appetite than others for this kind of second look at such things as decisions, plans, knowledge, and beliefs. In some cases, circumstances play a role in how much enthusiasm accompanies a willingness to open a closed book.

However, it also seems that each of us has a preset place along the scale—ranging from grudgingly to enthusiastically—when presented with an opportunity to retread old ground. Some of us are more risk averse than others, less inclined to move away from what we have, less inclined to give up the security of the status quo. These tendencies reflect a desire to avoid outcomes that might be characterized as:

regret

retract

recant

repudiate

reject

refute

recede

People on the other end of the scale, who are more open to launching a reconsideration, might do so with a different set of outcomes in mind:

reform

refresh

refine

renew

revive

reaffirm

restore

How do some folks end up being guided by the words in this last list?

If you acknowledge having made some mistakes along the way . . .

If you know that some of your expectations will turn out to be wrong . . .

If growth in mind and heart is important to you . . .

If "static" reminds you of death
and "fluid" characterizes your sense of the life around us . . .

Then you might be ready for an adventure in reopening.

Dust to Dust

When I hit retirement, I joined with a few friends
in creating a nature preserve,
the home for a conservation cemetery
where traditional burial—natural burial—
takes place in a natural setting.

Other friends asked, "What is that?" They asked "Why?"
Here's why:

We created a conservation cemetery because we want to care for the earth by reducing burial activities that damage our natural home.

Because we want to be faithful stewards of this creation, preserving and restoring the habitats we have inherited.

Because we want to strengthen community among family and friends beyond the time of death.

Because we want to alleviate financial burdens often imposed at the death of a loved one, often upon those least able to bear those costs.

Because we want to embrace ritual that honors and celebrates the mystery and power we encounter through death.

Because we want to take seriously the ancient teaching, "For you are dust, and to dust you shall return."

In all of this, we want to continue to explore the full meaning of the seventh act of corporal mercy, as we respond to the traditional call to *Bury the Dead*.

We Better Be On Our Way

We've seen stones that were not rolling and were gathering moss.
We've spent time in easy chairs and we know what "couch potato" means.
We've come upon stagnant water, where much of the life there was dying.

Newton's first law of motion tells us that an object at rest will stay at rest, unless acted upon by some other force.

If we are inclined to *not* let life pass us by, we can supply that other force—the force which will get us moving. I'm not talking about random motions, about moving for moving's sake. I am not interested in filling days and nights revving up the engines, in a big hurry to go most anywhere.

Newton's law also tells us that an object in motion continues moving in the same direction, unless acted upon by another force. We can also supply that force. If we are on our way, which way are we going to go?

We all serve purposes. Serving *a* purpose is different than serving *my* purpose. If we haven't chosen a purpose, we have been chosen by one. Many of us are dedicating our lives to purposes chosen for us—perhaps chosen by parents, spouses, or children; by friends, peers, or colleagues; by role models, bosses, advertisers, politicians, preachers, tweeters, instagrammers, or influencers.

My money-earning career spanned 35 years at the same university. Early on, I figured out that I did not want to reach age 65 and feel like my life was something that happened *to* me. So, I vowed to step back, every five years, and take a look at how things were going—with the purpose, each time, of deciding whether I wanted to stay in that job. And that's what I did for all of those 35 years, choosing my vocational direction over and over and over again.

There is a difference between being drafted to serve some purpose or another and crafting a life in which we pursue purposes of our own choosing. Rather than settling for random or mindless motion, we can bend our words and deeds toward our chosen path. Not just once, but again and again. Maybe even more often than once every five years.

All of us have limits. Some of our limits abide under our skin, others impinge upon us from our environment. As we are able, we can turn our face toward our chosen direction, and take a step in that direction. Where do we start? We live in a world of hurt, on an ocean of need. If we don't recognize that we're surrounded by opportunities, we haven't looked hard enough. There is always more to be done. As my friend Michael sings: "We better be on our way."

CREEDS

A creed is a fixed set of words. People repeat creeds as a way of giving voice to their beliefs and to connect themselves with communities—past and present—that share those articles of faith.

In many creeds, specific words are not optional; disciples are expected to speak them all, exactly as written. And if the fixed set of words does not precisely match the convictions of every adherent? It is an observable fact that some believers stand with their community and say only some of the words, or mumble their way through the creed, or even decline to say anything during the recitation.

Some seekers look for a different way to adhere to the spirit of the creed, while still honoring their connection to the community. These seekers create a rephrased version of the creed.

Like this one:

Nicene Creed

Traditional	Welch Rephrasing
We believe in one God, the Father, the Almighty, maker of heaven and earth, of all that is, seen and unseen,	We believe in a higher power, the creative force that sustains and nurtures humanity in ways beyond our understanding.
We believe in one Lord, Jesus Christ, the only Son of God, eternally begotten of the Father,	We believe that Jesus of Nazareth embodied the power of this force:

God from God, Light from Light,
true God from true God,
begotten, not made,
of one Being with the Father.
Through him all things were made.

For us and for our salvation
he came down from heaven:
by the power of the Holy Spirit
he became incarnate from the
Virgin Mary, and was made man.

For our sake he was crucified under
Pontius Pilate; he suffered death
and was buried.
On the third day he rose again
in accordance with the Scriptures;
he ascended into heaven and is seated
at the right hand of the Father.

He will come again in glory to judge the
living and the dead, and his kingdom
will have no end.

We believe in the Holy Spirit, the Lord,
the giver of life, who proceeds from
the Father and the Son. With the
Father and the Son he is worshipped
and glorified.

He has spoken through the Prophets.
We believe in one holy catholic and
apostolic Church.

extraordinarily able to grasp its
meaning,
He revealed this face of reality to
us in his life and teaching

Because he was human, like us,
through grace and mercy
he offers us access
to this incomprehensible power.

There are forces in our lives
that assault humanity,
bringing suffering, degradation,
and death.
Because of the strength of such
forces,
Jesus was rejected and killed.
But death did not silence his
voice.

Evil will not eradicate the good
that he showed us,
a good that lives
in us and through us.

The power of this creative force
is at work in our lives today.
Our foremothers and fathers
gave witness to this source of life
and goodness in their words and
deeds.
We, as members of this
community,
will likewise give witness
in our words and deeds.

We acknowledge one baptism for the
forgiveness of sins.
We look for the resurrection of the dead,
and the life of the world to come.

Amen.

Secure in our faith, we will fear
no evil.
When we falter, goodness and
mercy will rescue us.

Beyond our lives, grace will
abound.

Amen.

Unintended Consequences

Using maps is a conversation of sorts. The map speaks (especially in these days when digital maps are replacing paper ones). The map user listens, and then acts on what she has heard. Both sides of the transaction are crucial, the communication of information and the accurate reception. A breakdown on either side yields unintended consequences—like the time when I was driving a rental car in Europe and was surprised to find myself in France, apparently after making a wrong turn or two.

So, it takes two: a clear map and a competent reading. We know that this combination is still not enough to guarantee a "successful" trip. We call on Google Maps as we begin a long-distance drive. We set off with an expectation of where we are going and when we will get there. But: cars break down. Tires go flat. Detour signs appear. Bad weather impedes our progress. Sometimes we choose to modify the itinerary as a new attractive option presents itself.

If we are aware of such possibilities going in, we will be better equipped to cope when the map "fails" us.

As it is in our traveling life, so it is in our planning life. Doing a good job of charting an excellent course does not guarantee success. After all, we are talking about the future. I am reminded of the world maps that were produced several centuries ago. Back in those days, mapmakers had to contend with *terra incognita*, areas for which there was no information. They handled this problem in different ways—such as filling in with drawings of various figures or just leaving large areas blank.

Similar rigid limits on knowledge are in play when I am mapping my future. My maps are temporary. As pieces of the future become pieces of the present, I am continually revising maps, and sometimes revising destinations. In the meantime, I try to remember to be ready to cope with unintended consequences.

COMPANIONS

When I hear words of wisdom alone
I ponder them in silence.
When I hear them with a loved one
A conversation emerges.

When I eat a meal alone
My stomach is filled.
When I share a meal with a loved one
My soul is fed.

When I view nature's glory alone
My heart leaps.
When I view it with a loved one
Our hearts leap together.

When I am immersed in music alone
My mind goes to a beautiful elsewhere.
When I hear it with a loved one
We expand our shared memory.

When I travel beyond ordinary space
New vistas fill my senses.
When I travel with a loved one
A party for two breaks out.

When I am at home alone
The evenings can get long.
When I'm home with a loved one
The evenings can't get long enough.

When I face the future alone
I see nothing but unknownness.

When I face the future with a loved one
A known face accompanies me and brightens the way.

Who's a Liar?

It seems like nobody wants to be called a liar—although apparently this is not a strong preference, as we are surrounded by untruths. When someone is caught in a falsehood, the accused rarely confesses, such as, "Yep, you got me there. I lied." Sometimes they tell us that they misspoke, or they used a poor choice of words. These days, we are told that it wasn't a lie, only disinformation or alternative facts, or puffing. When they appear to have been caught dead to rights, before you know it, they just "walk it back."

Two of the more devious responses to charges of lying are the claims that the words were taken out of context or misconstrued. The fault, we are told, does not lie with the accused speaker, but with the listeners who just didn't get it right.

With deception being such a big business, why are we hesitant to call a liar a liar? Some possibilities that may create the hesitation:

    —"White lies" are seen as harmless.

    —Charges of lying can provoke retaliation (even lawsuits).

    —It's considered bad manners to call someone a liar.

    —Sometimes deceitful communication leads to results that are judged to be good.

Do we even have a common understanding of what a lie is? Perhaps we could a start with something like this: *a person lies when he intentionally deceives others by saying something that is not factually true.* Three elements: an intent to deceive, false content, and success in deceiving another.

Even if we set aside our increasing inability to agree on what is factually true, this three-point definition opens the way to a lot of "what ifs?" What if the deception resulted from an omission, or accidently, or through a statement that was technically true? Or, what if the untruth was the result of negligence, or was spoken in a context where deception is expected? If the attempt to deceive fails and no one was fooled, is that still a lie?

Who's a liar? It appears that answering this question is not a simple matter for some of us, some of the time, which, of course, complicates the effort to understand our world and to decide how to respond to it. Our current state of affairs gives us all the more reason to be on guard and to treasure those among us who do practice truth-telling.

GRATITUDE

If I could have one do-over, I believe I would use it to do a better job of expressing gratitude. Countless helping hands have contributed to forming my life along the way. I should have said "thank you" more often and more fully.

Late in life, I have tried to do better. But for many of my benefactors, it is too late. Many of them are dead. I have lost touch with many more . . . I don't even know if some of them are dead or alive.

This a poor substitute, but I want to take this opportunity to acknowledge some of those people who contributed to my life.

> —the family friend who, behind the scenes, made possible for me formative opportunities that my parents could never have afforded
>
> —the scout master who modeled a caring compassion for others
>
> —my college dorm mates who broadened my horizons
>
> —the priest who offered to me the most amazing retirement years

The fabulous teachers throughout my 22 years of formal education, including:

> —the Freshman English teacher who woke me up to the realization that I had a long way to go
>
> —the History teacher who taught me that just because I learned something first didn't make it right
>
> —the Ethics teacher who showed me what I wanted to do for the rest of my life

—the many bosses over the years who helped me develop
a useful skill set, even if occasionally they taught me by
modeling some things that I wanted to avoid

—so many, many colleagues and friends who have been
generous in their support, tolerant when I was slow, and
forgiving when I was wrong

—my brothers, who were my best friends and kept me
around the house while others my age were out and about
making some bad choices

—my parents, who embodied love for me. Every day.

Contemplative Justice

CONTEMPLATIVE

(reflective, thoughtful, seeking, deliberate, pursuing, exploring, searching)

JUSTICE

(fairness, impartiality, conscientious, equity, fair treatment, morality)

Contemplative Justice entails perpetual thinking and perpetual doing.

The Contemplative part is a matter of perpetual *thinking*: a careful, deliberative search for answers to the question: "What does Justice require?" In the flow of time, the question will be asked over and over. There are no canned answers to the question, no formulas that can be plugged in to produce a solution. The search is never over. The answer that suits the question in one place at one time may not fit in a different place and time.

The Justice part is a matter of perpetual *doing*. While the thinking task can be demanding, it pales in comparison to the job of making a society or a world more just.

We sign up for this duty, knowing that the job never ends. We understand that there will be no perfection in the knowing or in the doing. We also understand that the inevitable imperfection is no excuse for not doing the best we can.

I think of the search for justice as something like a continuous game of horseshoes. We try to get the shoe as close as we can to the stake with each throw. Getting close *does* count. Even better, occasionally we get a ringer. And then? Then we pick it up and throw again. Over and over. Each toss stands on its own. One ringer does not change the amount of effort that is required for the next throw. Three ringers in a row do not earn us retirement in this game without end. The game *is* never-ending, but I am not. My hope is that when someone steps in and takes my place, I will feel like I had made a contribution to the game.

A Mantra

Live Love.
Love Life.

Sung

I once heard Garrison Keillor read the lyrics to Bruce Springsteen's "Born in the USA" as a poem. Without the music, the words still felt powerful for me as Springsteen's musical rendition rang through my mind, accompanying Keillor's spoken presentation, note by note.

Songs are amazing, in part, because the music gives us clues about how to hear, how to feel, how to absorb the words.

I wondered how the reading of "Born in the USA" struck the listeners who were not acquainted with the powerful way that The Boss sang that song.

On the following pages, there are lyrics to some of my songs, also not accompanied here by their melodies. I trust that something of what I have in mind in these songs will come through, even without their tunes.

Love Doesn't Die

Love doesn't die when your body's buried in the ground.

What are we after, why are we here,
What does it matter when the end is always near?
What are we chasing, what is chasing us?
Are the questions worth our time before we return to dust?

What treasures should we pile up in our bank?
Which honors are the ones that show us where we rank?
Is it power and glory, is it wealth or fame?
Do the dollars and the prizes make up our remains?

Are we seeking happiness, pleasure over pain,
Making a life of comfort in our own domain?
Looking for a path that's safe, avoiding loss and fear,
Can we see beyond the walls in our days while we are here?

Can we find our answers in creeds we repeat
When we ignore the words to fit our own beliefs?
Are the answers in the books sitting on the shelves?
Can great teachers teach us how to answer for ourselves?
Maybe the answer's just as pure as loving others as yourself.

Love doesn't die when your body's buried in the ground.

Compass in Your Soul

My dad came home and told us boys what went down in that
East Texas town,
How he and Albert left the road when lunch time came around.
Hey there boy, the waitress called, the kitchen's where you'll find
your food.
Dad said that's not right. I will eat there too.

You don't need to hold your finger in the wind.
You don't have to know which way the breezes blow.
You've got a compass buried in your soul.
Deep down you know you've got a compass buried in your soul.

The Freedom Rides were off the road, the haters they had won
the day.
The students said let's get on board, but elders blocked the way.
The die was cast when John spoke up: we've got to see it to the
end.
If not us, then who? If not now, then when?

You don't need to hold your finger in the wind.
You don't have to know which way the breezes blow.
You've got a compass buried in your soul.
Deep down you know you've got a compass buried in your soul.

Strong winds are blowing once again, spreading fear and hate
across our land.
The center's weak, the Union's strained, some folks have got to
take a stand.
You don't need a weather vane, just heed words that were true
back then:

If not us, then who? If not now, then when?
If not us, then who? If not now, then when?

Always We Begin Anew

When the door clangs shut behind you, you feel the walls close
in,
You know it's just an hour for you, for him it never ends,
And you walk from the prison and you wonder how it goes from
here.

"I love you like a brother, but there's nothin' I can do,"
He said as he shows you the door.
As you walk off the job site, you wonder where you go from here.

Hard times are comin', the only question's when.
Once they're bangin' on your door, you gotta let 'em in.
Running and hiding won't bring peace to your soul
And turning your back only deepens the hole.
But always, always, always we begin anew.

You never think you'll hear the words: "I love someone else."
Your past becomes a big dead end.
As you're leaving your home, you wonder where you'll go from
here.

"I've stopped eating" she whispered, from her dying bed,
The end she hastens stops her pain, but your road lies ahead,
And you walk from the graveyard, and you wonder how you'll go
on from here.

Hard times are comin', the only question's when.
Once they're bangin' on your door, you gotta let 'em in.
Running and hiding won't bring peace to your soul
And turning your back only deepens the hole.

But always, always, always we begin anew.
Always, always, always we begin anew.

S L E E P W A L K I N G

It's Bill's life, it's so great,
He's in charge, he's got it made.
Climbs the ladder, never looks down,
No need to see what's going 'round.
Counts his dollars, keeping score,
All he needs is a little more.
But he is sleepwalking, sleepwalking through life.
Yes, he is sleepwalking, sleepwalking through life.

Days drift past, nights go by,
Time calls Jane to learn to fly.
The world is wide, and it's real,
It's her chance to touch and feel.
She could have jumped but she sits instead,
Her mind's stuck in the interweb.
Because she's sleepwalking, sleepwalking through life.
Yes, she is sleepwalking, sleepwalking through life.

See the people on life's trail . . . .
They're counting minutes, marking miles, losing all that time.
Headphones on and blinders too, missing Nature's rhyme,
One more day behind.

Walk the streets in a daze,
Pain and need are beyond my gaze.
Got my list of things to do.
Anything else? Don't have a clue.
First things first and I'm on my way,
Maybe I'll help another day.
And I am sleepwalking, sleepwalking through life.

134

Can we stop sleepwalking, sleepwalking through life?
Sleepwalking through life.

135

MY SMALL WORLD

The headlines tell the story of those children he gunned down.
Quickly scan the text to see was this in our own town.
Was it here? Was it close? Is the blood nearby?
We're lucky all this happened on the world's other side.
Nevermind. Nevermind.

New forecasts of nature's woes make the TV news.
Do the facts before our eyes mean it's time to choose?
Rising seas are in our future, that's when we'll find a way.
We'll take the road to save our home, but not yet today.
Nevermind. Nevermind.

The nation's running off the track, do leaders really care?
Can I find a role to play, helping make things fair?
Those on top call the shots, keeping others down.
In this world of power and fame, my voice would hardly count.
Nevermind. Nevermind.

Where I Want To Be

I had a dream last night; it was very fine.
I saw a place, so sublime, where I could live my life.
A place without despair, that's where I want to be.

All the cats and dogs play together well.
The home team wins, every game, and the dishes wash them-
selves.
The lawn is always green, that's where I want to be.

> It's a dream I know.
>
> We're not even close.
>
> The dreams are here
>
> to show us where
>
> we should go.

The children mind their q's and p's, schools have made them
tame.
Our nation's leaders get along because they're all the same.
I am always right, that's where I want to be.

You never have to worry, never need to strive.
All the things surrounding you, always turn out right.
Vacation every day, that's where I want to be.

No alarms are set, to jar us awake,
Cause I don't see in this place a difference I could make.
All the good's been done, that's where I want to be.

> One question I see,
>
> Is that really,

I mean really,
Is that really where
I want to be?

I'M WITH YOU

When I wake to the rooster's call, I'm with you.
Dozing off at midnight's strike, I'm with you.
When you end my sayings, when I think your thoughts,
All those ways we make a home, I'm with you.

When three highways come between us, I'm with you.
When we travel different paths, I'm still with you.
Vapor trails are all I see, as you fly from me . . . .
Always I wait you here, I'm with you.

How did we get here I don't know.
Don't have a clue to find that road.
Don't really know where the answers are,
But I'm damn sure how I want to start,
Just hold me close.

When my mind strays far away, I'm with you.
You see black and I see white, I'm still with you.
You say yes and I say no, it seems we're apart . . .
But the matters that count are deep down in our hearts,
And that is how . . . I am with you.

Come On Love

The table holds a silent phone staring back at me.
One more night, captive still, I wish that I could be free.
The door's not locked, no bars I see, yet I can barely breathe.
I cannot move, I can't escape the hold she has on me.

Gloom engulfs this empty room, walls are pressing in.
Nothing ventured, nothing gained, that rattles in my brain.
Easy to hear, harder to do, an order way too tall.
And so I sit here frozen still, hoping she will call.

Come on Love, please put up a fight,
Come on Love, can you save my life?
Come on Love, come on Love, come on Love and save my heart
this time.

I wonder how she's doing now, is she bound like me?
Could I end her painful doubt if I could just break free?
Does her phone torment her, staring her down as well?
Does my weakness, does my fear, create her own hell?

Come on Love, please put up a fight,
Come on Love, can you save my life?
Come on Love, come on Love, come on Love and save our hearts
this time.

Postscript

Always words fall short
of giving proper shape to
the things we love most

Postscript

This book is not finished. If I stay true to the book's spirit, it will never be finished.

Every time I have read through this collection, I have made changes. I have played with some of these pieces many times. The moment of publication does not mark the arrival at the finish line. Rather, putting these words in print reflects a judgment that they are good enough. For now . . .

I hope that I will always keep space open for new thoughts and new ways to express these thoughts. If Opening Thoughts become frozen in place, they might begin to feel like Sound Bites.

The more we look, the more likely it is that we will find new possibilities. The "more" is not just about quantity . . . how many times we look . . . how long we look. The "more" is about intensity, about how committed we are to this continuing pilgrimage to other places.

Let's stay on the move.

Author's Thanks

First, to Celeste, my wife and best friend, who has accompanied me on this path as advisor, reviewer, critic, booster, and foremost as loving companion.

To Becca Stevens and Rebecca Wells, who have provided counsel, guidance, and encouragement, from before my first thought of writing this book until it was done.

To Kendall Hinote, dispenser of wisdom and tireless partner as we turned a pile of words into the finished product that you are holding in your hands.

To more friends (in alphabetical order) who have read my work and have given me feedback that made this product better: Tom Angland, Bert Baily, cj Casciotta, Carolyn Goddard, Carole Hagan, Keith Hagan, Virginia Scott, Gay Welch, and Bonnie Smith Whitehouse.

To the Center for Contemplative Justice for joining me in this adventure. Thank you, Scott Owings.

To You, the Reader. Writing is only half of the experience. Without you, I would only have a stack of paper taking up space on a shelf at home.

The Center for Contemplative Justice

The Center for Contemplative Justice grows and sustains corporal acts of justice arising from contemplation. Since 2004, the not for profit has worked to support people's common life of prayer and service. The center does this by building community and deeper conversation through events, pilgrimages, publications, and service. The center nurtures the contemplative life and supports visions for social and structural change. This book is our first foray into publication, and we hope that it sparks new insights and actions to celebrate contemplation and justice. We have loved partnering with Don Welch.

The center provides administrative and financial resources to individuals and groups. Among the recipients of CCJ support are: Escuela Anne Stevens (San Eduardo, Ecuador), Center for Urban Economic Justice (Nashville), Holy Cross Hospice (Gaborone, Botswana), Mindfulness in Nashville Education, and Larkspur Conservation, which is practicing natural burial in nature preserves in Tennessee.

Becca Stevens, Chair
Scott Owings, President
tcfcj.org

About the Author

Don Welch spends his time volunteering in the non-profit world and writing, after three decades of teaching ethics in the Law School and the Divinity School at Vanderbilt University. He is the author of five previous books, the most recent of which is *A Guide to Ethics and Public Policy: Finding Our Way*. Don and his wife, Celeste, live in Nashville where they go outdoors habitually, naturally.